TO PETER:
MAY YOU ALWAYS
HAVE   SAFE

havens
EXOTIC **hideaways** and

Yo.   ROSS

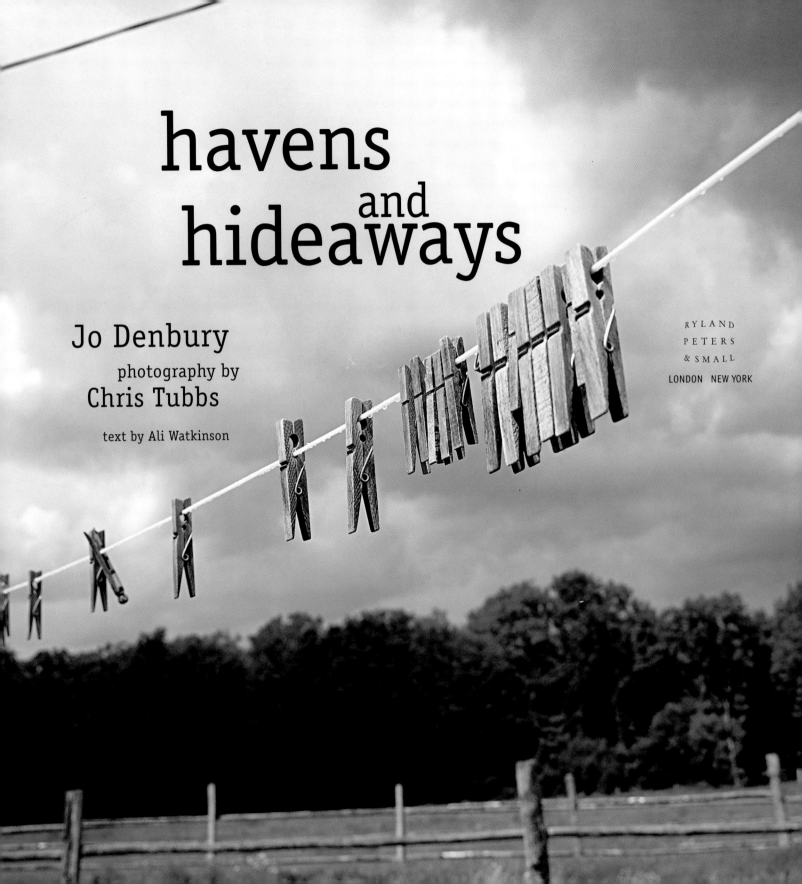

havens
and
hideaways

Jo Denbury

photography by
Chris Tubbs

text by Ali Watkinson

RYLAND
PETERS
& SMALL
LONDON   NEW YORK

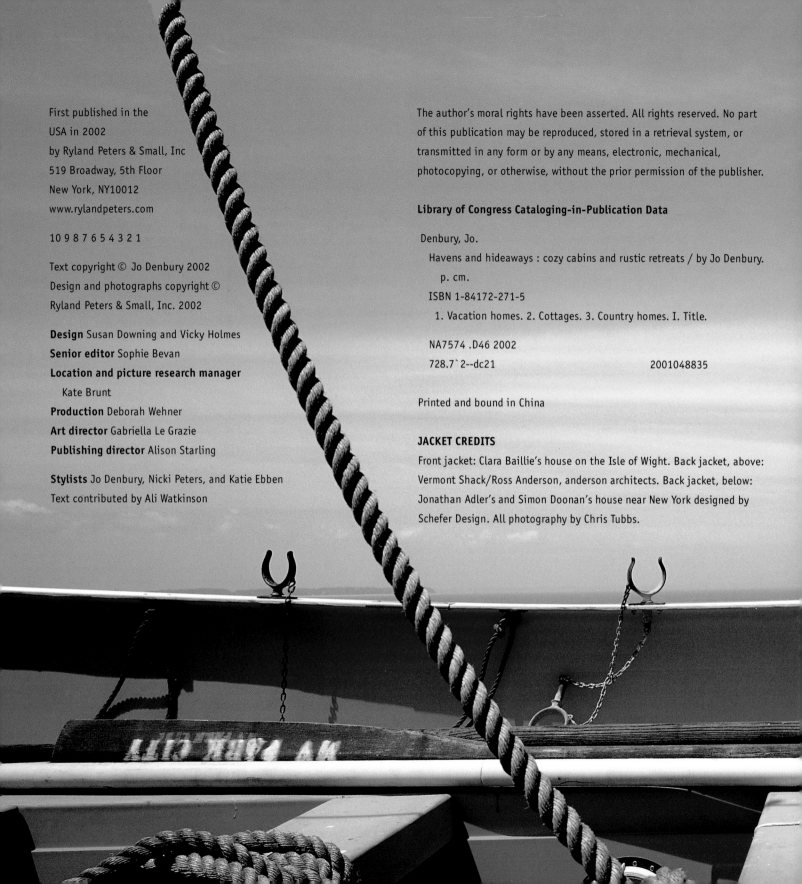

First published in the
USA in 2002
by Ryland Peters & Small, Inc
519 Broadway, 5th Floor
New York, NY10012
www.rylandpeters.com

10 9 8 7 6 5 4 3 2 1

Design Susan Downing and Vicky Holmes
Senior editor Sophie Bevan
Location and picture research manager
   Kate Brunt
Production Deborah Wehner
Art director Gabriella Le Grazie
Publishing director Alison Starling

Stylists Jo Denbury, Nicki Peters, and Katie Ebben
Text contributed by Ali Watkinson

Library of Congress Cataloging-in-Publication Data

Denbury, Jo.
   Havens and hideaways : cozy cabins and rustic retreats / by Jo Denbury.
      p. cm.
   ISBN 1-84172-271-5
      1. Vacation homes. 2. Cottages. 3. Country homes. I. Title.

   NA7574 .D46 2002
   728.7`2--dc21   2001048835

Printed and bound in China

JACKET CREDITS

Front jacket: Clara Baillie's house on the Isle of Wight. Back jacket, above: Vermont Shack/Ross Anderson, anderson architects. Back jacket, below: Jonathan Adler's and Simon Doonan's house near New York designed by Schefer Design. All photography by Chris Tubbs.

contents

introduction

This is a subject that I have been thinking about for a long time, about creating a home that is rooted in our primal instincts. Why? Because I enjoy the rituals of life: making fires, growing vegetables, bathing outdoors, being able to see the stars.

As a child, I lived for a period of time in a house without electricity, and I make no bones about the necessity (and luxury) of mod cons—it is no fun being cold and without power. But what I have noticed is that a lot of us are feeling out of sync with ourselves because we have lost the very essence of what makes us tick. This book is not meant as answer, but more as inspiration. We are living in an era where we increasingly question how we are spending our time. After all, we are born explorers and questers after the unknown, and we spend a lot of time pacing the perimeter of life, searching for the answers.

My belief is that it is the very "high-tech jungle" we have created for ourselves that prevents us from finding these answers. Six thousand years ago humans depended on the elements for his life, and today nothing has changed: our bodies are warmed by the sun, our lungs constantly refilled with air, and our vitality depends on taking in water and the fruits of the land. Yet we live in a time when we feel detached from these necessities. Witness the rise in vacations that take us "back to basics"—what are we searching for if it isn't to live at one, even for a short period of time, with nature?

The more we embrace technology and material comforts, the more part of us yearns

for an altogether simpler existence, one that shrugs off modern-day excesses and returns to a way of life which is part of the natural landscape. There is a simple joy to be found in witnessing the cycle of the seasons, knowing the first frost and, better still, tasting vegetables that have come straight from the earth.

In the future, we will work out what our needs really are. Wage-slavery will be a thing of the past as we realize its futility and the importance of balance in our lives and our homes. Time is the greatest and most valuable commodity of our century, yet we have lost the moment to pause and marvel. This book is about getting back to experiencing the textures of life. This doesn't require huge quantities of money—a recycled railroad wagon, an old shack, or a boat can all give you space to find time.

Many of the people whose hideaways are featured in these pages talk of a need for solitude, escape, contrast, quiet, emptiness; to be closer to the earth, the weather and the sky, and to feel time. This book is intended as an act of celebration for those who have crossed the divide, and an act of inspiration to those who have yet to go.

water

why water?

Water is vital to all life: it quenches our thirsts, cleanses our bodies, soothes our minds, and restores our spirits.

The element of water has long been venerated. A century before the Greek philosopher Empedocles directed that the universe was made up of four elements, his fellow thinker, Thale had named water as the ultimate substance; the principal of all things. Its position as a super-element is understandable, given its importance to life, and its omnipresence. We, and much of the natural world around us, would not exist without water—our bodies are 70 percent water—and water covers more than two-thirds of the earth's surface.

Luckily for us, water is, without adverse interference, endlessly recyclable. As every schoolchild knows, it rains, rivers form, they flow into the sea, the surface of the sea evaporates, clouds form, and, once again, it rains ....

However, as the water conservation expert Peter Warshall eloquently writes, there is more than sustenance in water, there is bounteous pleasure, too. "Water is more than a commodity .... Sloshing around in tanks and oxbows, swimming pools, and creeks nurtures giggles, sitting by the ocean quiets the soul and steam baths and jacuzzis hold unexplained healing powers of water. In our dreams, reflections, and stories, water as perhaps no other substance gushes with beauty, spirit, grace, and stories of long-term community life."

As each of these hideaways proves, there is an undeniable romance to being by the water, and perhaps even more so when we are actually *on* the water. One of the havens here is a barge that the owner sails each summer from its city mooring to a rural estuary. By contrast, another is a village dwelling, high above the sea, yet its owner has created an atmosphere where you can almost feel the swell of the sea and half expect to see Tangiers harbor coming into view.

healing, sensual
mesmerizing
cooling, fluid
invigorating
dissolving, reflective
revitalizing
purifying, calming

textures, colors, patinas
by the water

Water has a surprising number of forms—think of all the words we need to describe them: "river," "pool," "waterfall," "trickle," "snowflake," "ocean," "cloud," "glacier," are just a few—and it appears in as many colors.

This endlessly varying character and palette may inspire poets, but it is only with the benefit of science that we can explain why frozen water should be white, and why one sea seems blue and another green. The sea commonly looks blue because water molecules absorb red light and scatter blue light back to our eyes. Areas of the ocean that reflect blue light from the sky will look bluer than areas that reflect white light from clouds. Yet chlorophyll from microscopic plants or the reflection of yellow light from sand in shallow water can both tinge the sea green. Where water droplets or ice crystals are present, they scatter light of all colors, sending white light to our eyes.

Whether a frozen pond or a limpid pool, the foam on the surf or droplets in the air, the texture of water is cooling and refreshing, shiny and wet, sensuously satiny. Its texture is also found in the pebbles worn smooth by the ocean and driftwood carved into fantastical abstract shapes; it is damp, mossy banks beside a stream, sharp wet rocks underfoot, and the patina left by salty air beating against our dwellings.

ocean, wedgwood
peacock blue
midnight, sky
delft, thistle
slate, cobalt
sapphire, cornflower
indigo,
powder blue, dusty
marshmallow
smooth, slippery
chalky, ivory

decorate your space with
water in mind

Just as water is cooling and soothing to the touch, using it as inspiration for the decoration of our homes can create a similar effect for our eyes and our minds.

The colors of water—white, myriad shades of blue and blue-green, and silvery metallics—are shades that suggest tranquillity and space. People are often afraid of these shades, believing they can make a room seem cold. But think of how deliciously inviting a still pool of water or a calm sea looks on a scorching day—hold that color in your mind's eye—and be inspired to choose a singing shade that enhances and plays with the light. Nothing could be cheerier or more redolent of summer.

Blue and white is a classic combination; think of the sky and clouds and the white spray on energetic waves. It is a squeaky clean, resolutely nautical style. For a modern update, pair blue with smooth, silvery metallics. Or be inspired by the textures and colors of shells and pebbles on the beach and age-worn stones along riverbanks, to match blue with tactile gray, ecru, beige, and sandy fabrics and accessories—rough linen, hemp, and seagrass matting, for instance—for a more forgiving, less pristine look.

Alternatively, let blue take a back seat and just use it as an accent color in your scheme. See how it clamors for attention, bringing structure to an otherwise neutral background, just as the smallest patch of sea glimpsed from miles inland catches our eye.

"Blue and green should not be seen"—so goes the old saying—but think of where those two shades overlap and use shades of turquoise, from deep greenish-blue through to palest aquamarine, to conjure up memories of oceans stormy and deep or shallow and tropical.

ISLAND
SHELTER

Why, if we have a fundamental need for personal space, do we deny ourselves the opportunity to escape the city for good? It seems that just as a sauna and plunge pool wouldn't be as refreshingly invigorating or intensely soothing without the other for contrast, a haven could not be such without a completely contrasting existence to escape from.

We may struggle against the challenges of "real life," but most of us would be lost without them. As the anthropologist Desmond Morris says, "the city, despite all its faults, acts as a giant stimulus-centre where our great inventiveness can flourish and develop." A jet-setting New York ceramicist, the owner of this island retreat was seeking "a mellow, happy getaway; a place for my partner to write, me to make pottery, and our Norfolk terrier— Liberace—to gambol; somewhere quite different from the insanity of New York."

"We chose this area because it is only a short ferry crossing from Long Island, yet once you're on the boat you feel totally remote and cut off from things. The minute I'm on the water I feel like I'm on vacation—it acts like a moat, isolating us from our hectic lives. By the time we arrive on the island, we are effectively misanthropic shut-ins—to the extent that we become almost feral, barely even bothering to wash or get dressed! We cook, chill, frolic, and take dips on the deserted beach and that's about it."

While the haven is used as often as possible—usually for three-day weekends—his lifestyle here is, tellingly, not one that he would be comfortable with on a permanent basis, preferring to be able to chop from this Robinson Crusoe existence to its complete opposite, a well-groomed one in frenetic New York. "We would love to spend a month or so

Cedar decking rings the house, forming a gentle link between the pristine interior and the deer-inhabited woods beyond. A wood stove in the living room creates a dramatic focal point and provides the only source of heat. The owners created the quirky fireplace from found stones and pebbles.

on the island—the most we can ever manage is a couple of weeks—but I couldn't live there all year round. There's no culture for one thing, and when I say we're 'feral,' I don't mean that feral!"

While the real estate agents describe the house as having "winter water views," the bay is less than a minute's walk away, and it is possible to canoe literally from the doorstep via the creek that runs by the house. "We're constantly on or by the water, swimming, plopping our kayaks into the creek, or throwing the dog into the bay. The water is a constant, reassuring presence."

Bought as a one-bedroom, one-bathroom shack with a gallery, what originally captivated the owner was the property's sense of openness and airiness. Intriguingly, rumor had it that the original structure was built in 1972 by a Pan Am pilot from a kit. Architects were retained to create a simple master bedroom and bathroom extension, "so that we could have our own haven within the hideaway."

"A sample of
the country
does the
city good."
Joseph Roux

Having explored the potential in geodesic domes and Airstream trailers to provide the extra sleeping space they needed for guests, the owners finally commissioned architects to create an extension. The horizontal windows in the resulting master bedroom were designed to give privacy while allowing an eye-level panorama of the enveloping leaves and branches, a sort of living wallpaper.

The new part of the house was designed to maintain the handmade, unpretentious quality of the existing A-frame building, which suits the relaxed style of the owners and the working-class island, a place very different from the nearby Hamptons. Simple, natural materials like plywood and stone have been given a low-key, subtle textural role by the uniform paint scheme. The blanket covering of white gloss paint hides a multitude of sins, bringing together a hodgepodge of disparate materials and styles to create a clean and airy atmosphere that is unthreateningly modern. It also provides a blank canvas against which to display more homey, personal elements, like the owner's own pottery and a bedspread featuring a giant snail shell which he made specially for the house. It's a look the owner describes as "modern rustic." For the architects, who are now regular visitors, "it is a very grounded, down-to-earth house; somewhere you immediately feel at home." For the owner the atmosphere is "above all happy and childlike."

"Living on a boat gives new meaning to the phrase 'high maintenance,'" says the owner of this 86-foot (26-meter) traditional Thames sailing barge, "as there is always something that needs repairing or painting or greasing."

But it is worth the effort for the joy of a peaceful riverside life. "It's so quiet; it's like being in the countryside, and friends liken visits to being on vacation. Sitting on the deck with a beer, the effect is instantly calming. It's fascinating to live so close to the natural rhythms of the river and sea."

Unusually, this boat is both a city home and a country retreat, for, unlike most of the surrounding houseboats, it is seaworthy. At the beginning of every summer, the owner dismantles the huge mast—so it can clear the many bridges across the river safely—and takes the barge down

The barge was a working boat until 1970 when it was converted into a houseboat and its hold was divided into several rooms. When the present owner acquired it, he removed the partitions to reinstate the hold as one vast loftlike, wood-lined space. As wood is an incredibly efficient insulator, the boat remains cozy throughout the winter, an effect enhanced by the warm pinkish-red used for the "lining."

SAILING
BARGE

protective

tactile

rhythmic

swaying

creaking

flowing

therapeutic

R.C.

In the bow of the boat is a built-in bunk (opposite) in traditional style. At the other end of the space is a salvaged cast-iron bathtub. Woods of varying ages add character—the floor, actually the "ceiling" in sailing lingo, is Douglas fir, and the sides are oak and pitch pine.

the coast to a village on the estuary of the River Medway. Here he moors it for four or five months, staying with friends in London during the week and driving down at weekends for sailing parties.

The boat encourages an outdoor life. Its deck is a cheery place to watch the world go by, reclining in the hammock strung between the mast and the shroud. Barbecues, among the anchor and piles of rope, are a regular feature; and sleeping under the stars on a summer night is especially soothing. "What's really nice about living on the barge is that my home is transportable. Sometimes I can be down in the hold in my familiar quarters, and it is only when I come up on deck—and feel a moment of surprise on seeing new surroundings—that I remember my 'home' has moved many miles from London to a secluded estuary on the coast."

SUMMER
HOUSE

Thoughfully positioned to look out through a natural break in the surrounding copse, this elegant summerhouse enjoys uninterrupted views far out to sea.

"There is a magical stillness about this place that takes you away from real life. I couldn't imagine anywhere more perfect," declares the owner with heartfelt passion.

Inspired to create a haven by a childhood love of beach huts, she chose a site on the boundary of her large, overrun garden. Sheltered from behind by an ancient, towering yew tree, the wooden hut nestles in a wooded glade. Lawn and flowerbeds wrap around three sides, while directly in front, further emphasizing its connection with water, the owner dug a pond. "I wanted it to feel as if the summerhouse was floating above the water."

Prompted by the simple dwellings seen on a visit to the west coast of Scotland—where scarce building materials are religiously recycled—the owner sourced reclaimed materials from all over the island where she lives. "I wanted the summerhouse to blend in completely with its surroundings,

so I searched through vast piles of assorted timber to find just what I wanted. I eventually came across old gable boards from a stone house that was being demolished. The old doors are French; they were in a poor state with no glass, but then I came across sheets of beautiful old stained glass in pale shades of blue, pink, green, and yellow, and cut out sections to be set into the corners of the doors and windows. When the sun shines through the glass, the colors dance on the wall behind." The roof of the summerhouse is covered with cedar shingles that quickly faded to a warm silvery-gray to blend with the distressed exterior. "We thought about painting the outside," says the owner, "but as the structure took shape, it seemed to settle into the landscape, and visitors say it looks as though it has been here forever."

It was important to the owner to position the summerhouse where it would be central to plant life and visiting wildlife. "We love to stand on the seemingly unsupported veranda leaning out over the pond. There is a deep area for water lilies and a shallow area for marginal aquatics, which need to be restricted so we do not lose the reflections from the oaks and yew trees nearby. Pond skaters, water beetles, toads, and dragonflies quickly discovered and colonized it."

soft
faded
simple
welcoming
reclaimed
bygone
daydreams
time

Above all, a haven must be cozy. Here, reclaimed materials, a comfy old sofa, and gently faded florals lend an old-fashioned, genteel air suggesting that not only has it been here forever, but that afternoon tea will be served any minute.

The inside has been painted a soft, sea-washed, turquoise blue that positively vibrates in the generous light and connects the summerhouse with the colors of the sea and sky that fill the horizon. Electricity and water are installed, and an old French wood-burning stove provides heat. The double doors were designed to open fully so it is possible to watch the sun rise directly opposite.

"The light streams in off the sea, and you wake incredibly early. Here we're witness to all the changing moods of the sea and the sky, and are surrounded by the sounds of the sea lashing in storms and the early morning bird song. Our time here definitely heightens our awareness of things like the colors of the seasons and the earthiness of a simple place."

MEDITERRANEAN
CALM

Occasionally we need to be alone or, at least, alone with our thoughts. Solitude should be a straightforward state to achieve, but in reality something so simple and natural is often impossible given the demands of our lifestyles.

As the psychiatrist Anthony Storr has written, "...the capacity to be alone is necessary if the brain is to function at its best. Human beings easily become alienated from their own deepest needs and feelings. Learning, thinking, innovation, and maintaining contact with one's own inner world are all facilitated by solitude."

Sentiments with which the Italian owner of this tiny, vibrantly decorated house in Provence would undoubtedly agree. Hers is a haven to be completely alone in while escaping the humid summers of Milan. "I go there to relax. Without my husband, 96-year-old mother, daughter, dog, cats, and clients! I need and like to be by myself from time to time."

Her days here are spent on the terrace reading, drawing, and painting. The only social contact comes from visiting the market of the traditional

The owner painted the walls herself. "In decoration I am inspired most by artefacts—their faded colors and their history—like the antique ceramic tiles from Portugal which I have used in a patchwork effect on the stairs and in the kitchen area, and the Turkish carpet which suggested the colors for the living room."

hill town or, in the evening, sitting in the doorway, chatting with her neighbor. Only rarely does she meet friends. "I am happy to be by myself for days and days and really do nothing very much at all. I find it wonderfully relaxing."

Squeezed into the ancient town walls, the house is unusually long and narrow—roughly 23 feet (7 meters) deep by 8 feet (2.5 meters) wide. Inspired by its boatlike proportions, the owner decided to treat the decoration of the small house as if it were a seagoing craft and furnished it with treasures she had collected from all around the Mediterranean.

Most of the things are old or reclaimed, and come with a story and a patina of use and wear that sit well in the centuries-old house. Booty includes a carpet from Turkey, lights from Morocco, an Arabian screen above the bed, and antique ticking fabric from France. From farther afield are fabrics and furniture from India.

Bright chalky wall colors like cobalt and turquoise—the owner's trademark as a interior decorator—work well in the sunny climate of the Mediterranean. Restricting their use to below dado height and pairing them with white prevents the strong colors from dominating and making the tiny space look even smaller.

In the main living area, colorful Greek-style mattresses, stacked with bolsters and pillows, have been placed along each side, doubling as sofas and bunk beds—when visitors are allowed—and there is a tiny galley kitchen. The owner's bed on the floor above is set—boat style—into an alcove and acts as her "very own haven." At night the gleam from a nearby lighthouse shines in the open terrace doors and washes across the bedroom ceiling. All that spoils the sailing illusion is the house's lofty elevation, some 1,300 feet (400 meters) above the sparkling Côte d'Azur.

It could be said that the owner is a fair-weather sailor, since this is a haven just for the summertime when she spends up to two months here — the weather is continuously sunny and a good breeze from the mountains "ventilates" the tiny house. She is attached to her personal hideaway, but pragmatic, too, about the disadvantages of living here full time: "I like village life, but not the whole year round. In the winter, the winds are very strong and cold, and none of the houses are heated." So that is the time she returns to her city life, fortified by her time of solitude.

"How gracious, how benign, is Solitude." William Wordsworth

The owner only required a tiny kitchen in which to prepare simple meals, like salads ("I really don't like to cook!" she confesses). By squeezing it into the corner of the living room, space was freed up on the floor above for a boat-style bedroom and a bathroom overlooking the terrace. The French reclaimed zinc bathtub was cut in half and shortened to fit the space. "It's the most comfortable tub I've ever used," enthuses the owner, "it's like an armchair."

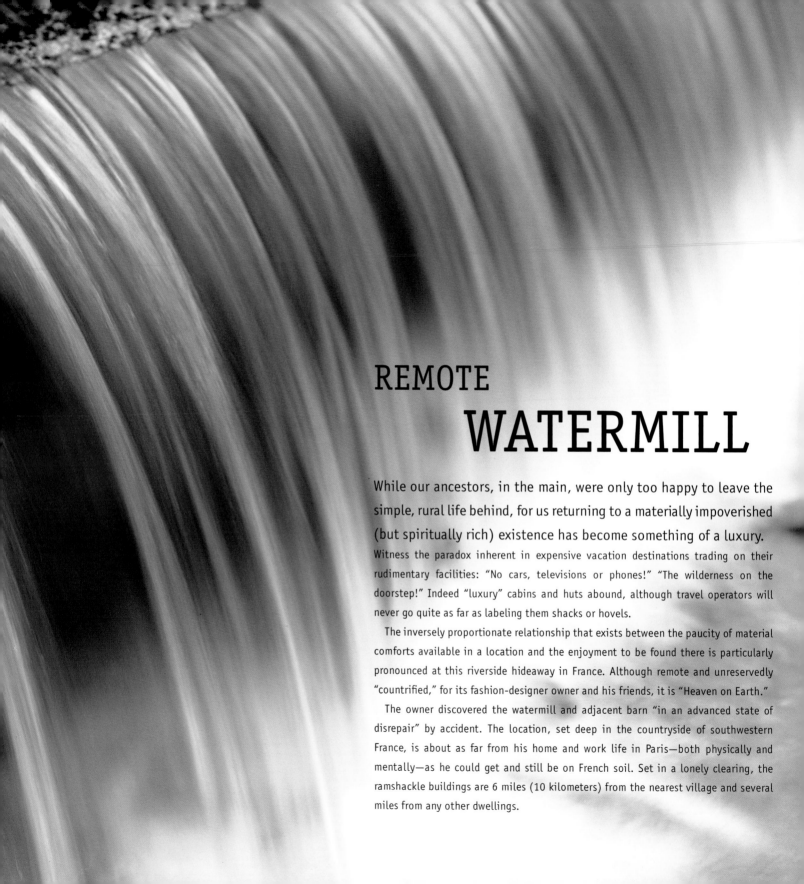

REMOTE
WATERMILL

While our ancestors, in the main, were only too happy to leave the simple, rural life behind, for us returning to a materially impoverished (but spiritually rich) existence has become something of a luxury. Witness the paradox inherent in expensive vacation destinations trading on their rudimentary facilities: "No cars, televisions or phones!" "The wilderness on the doorstep!" Indeed "luxury" cabins and huts abound, although travel operators will never go quite as far as labeling them shacks or hovels.

The inversely proportionate relationship that exists between the paucity of material comforts available in a location and the enjoyment to be found there is particularly pronounced at this riverside hideaway in France. Although remote and unreservedly "countrified," for its fashion-designer owner and his friends, it is "Heaven on Earth."

The owner discovered the watermill and adjacent barn "in an advanced state of disrepair" by accident. The location, set deep in the countryside of southwestern France, is about as far from his home and work life in Paris—both physically and mentally—as he could get and still be on French soil. Set in a lonely clearing, the ramshackle buildings are 6 miles (10 kilometers) from the nearest village and several miles from any other dwellings.

The singing blue paint that has been used inside and out is a traditional color associated with the wood treatment Bleu Charette, a pastelike by-product of the production of woad—once a common dye crop in Europe—which is not only beautiful, but a natural insect repellent to boot.

"The place is very isolated, and it's a big effort to get there. But the remoteness is a very important part of being there. I like the quiet and emptiness and relative silence—living in a city for most of the year I particularly appreciate the silence!"

Little has changed on this site since the buildings were erected in the early 1800s. The converted mill and barn have been simply furnished. "I enjoy the fact that the buildings originally had a practical, functional use. That they weren't designed for habitation means I have a lot of freedom to live here the way I want. I like empty spaces around me, so the layout is completely open plan, and consequently the views from inside are wide-ranging. I have deliberately not 'decorated' the buildings, just put in country furnishings and large pieces of furniture whose simplicity appeals to me."

Although the watermill hasn't operated in 25 years or more, for eleven months of the year the water still courses under and next to the mill, creating "a serene rocking impression," and acting as a sort of seasonal and meteorological barometer. "The river changes from season to season, yet is always a strong presence and a source of calm. In high summer it regularly dries up to little more than a trickle. But being in the south, the weather can change very quickly, the river bed suddenly fills with water from rain in far-off hills, and the yard can flood in no time."

cobalt

remote

rustic

sociable

simple

informal

understated

Ironically, given the lack of neighbors and the distance from civilization, socializing with friends is a very important aspect of life at this haven. "I have lots of visitors here. Often six or so people at a time, and more for special holidays. Everyone does as they please—playing music, reading, chatting, or eating long, lazy lunches. There are books everywhere and big armchairs."

Surrounded by dense plantings of oak and Judas trees, vines, ferns, roses, clematis, hydrangeas, and lilies, the buildings appear submerged in the abundant growth. "The house is in a garden, rather than having a garden around the house," comments the owner, who describes the barn as "like a boat set in grass." In the vegetable patch zucchini, peppers, tomatoes, and lots of herbs are grown for the kitchen. Cooking is an important pastime, and the owner loves to work in the kitchen

Natural materials have an affinity and sympathy with each another. Here, roughly hewn stone and timber for the buildings, clay for pottery, wicker for furniture, and paints made from natural pigments, sit comfortably with one another, achieving a timeless grace and "rightness."

Both the watermill and the barn situated alongside (seen here) have been simply furnished and decorated in accordance with their functional origins. A palette of white, gray, and soft blue has been used on the mismatched woodwork to create a harmonious effect that steers clear of looking overly contrived.

"with the doors and windows thrown wide open" so he can continue conversations with friends outside.

Given his connection with the fashion industry, the owner's desire for "somewhere to be calm and enjoy a timetable-free rhythm," somewhere away from sophistication and formality, is, perhaps, understandable. Three months here every year give him the opportunity to "do nothing but look, live, cook with produce from the garden, and listen to the silence and the sounds of the water running next to the house, the birds, trees, and nature all around."

WHITEWASHED
BEACH HUT

The poet Carl Sandberg wrote "Light and air and food and love and some work are enough." And so they are—the simple pleasures of this beach house perched on the southern coast of England satisfy its owners.

Two ladies commissioned this hut to be built in the 1930s as an escape by the sea. 50 years later, they lent it to the current owners—an artist and a local teacher—who eventually bought it from the ladies, now in their late eighties, a couple of years ago.

"The opportunity to have a second nest was a dream come true. We knew that in this place we would find peace, solitude, and a return to a simple life associated with childhood vacations. Even after just a day there I return refreshed and feel as though I have had a proper break. Staying there gives us the chance to spend some time together unencumbered by extraneous influences from a busy life, and our time there is very much battery charging. No road passes by, and the signals for cellphones are often weak because of weather conditions. The silence is broken only by the sound of the waves and the cries of the seagulls."

As with so many hideaways, the location is everything. The wooden hut stands right on the coastal path, on a large plot of land with 180-degree views of the sea immediately below. The beach is part of a 25-mile (40-kilometer) bank of stones and pebbles on the southern coast

Being so close to the sea, the exterior of the hut (opposite) requires regular maintenance—an ongoing labor of love—to protect it against the destructive forces of wind and salt. Pebbles are the sea's own handicrafts, tactile and enduringly beautiful. Displayed on ledges (this page), they are ready-made works of art.

of England. Positioned on low brick pillars, the fierce winds that sometimes batter the coast seem to dissipate underneath. "The winter and early spring weather can be very dramatic with huge waves and frightening storms. In summer, conversely, the area enjoys an almost subtropical microclimate."

The area is a magnet for migratory birds. "Little terns have a well-established summer colony here, and last year we had large numbers of clouded yellow butterflies blown over from France. We often see deer in the fields, and a large dog fox regularly patrols past at dusk. There are wild flowers in abundance along the banks including horned poppies, sea cabbage, sea thrift, alliums, and viper's bugloss. Our most exciting sight so far was a dolphin just off the coast."

Despite the wooden chalet's diminutive size and simplicity, the owners find they want for nothing. In the kitchen, the 1930s hutch (below) has been kept. It maintains the retro look and provides a place for everything from storage to a fold-down surface for chopping and serving.

light
sunshine
fresh air
white paint
fire-engine red
utilitarian
compact
powder blue
retro

Splashes of color—red to help warm and cheer the rooms on cold winter days, "when the sea and sky are the color of slate," says the owner, and blues to recall the more summery tones of the sky and sea—prevent the all-white space from looking stark.

The rhythm of the sea is a constant presence. "I am someone who has always needed to be near the sea. It keeps me sane and allows me to live my other life in a more productive way. The light is unlike what you would find inland, and the sunsets are spectacular. We take the same walk every morning and evening, and often stop to marvel at the power of the water. Here the sea is dangerously deep and the weather can change very quickly. When there is no wind and the sea is calm, though, it is like a gift, the light turns the sea bright turquoise, and you can swim in safety."

The hut is south facing, making the most of the sunlight from dawn until dusk. Even in winter months, light pours in. To maintain the feeling of light and to bring

simplicity to what is a small space, the hut is painted white throughout. Using white on the walls and ceilings also has the effect of making them recede so the rooms seem larger. Venetian blinds offer an adjustable solution to too much sunlight. The chalet has been kept much as it was in the 1930s. The original furniture remains. Having being designed for the space, it suits the retro style of the chalet and the proportions of the rooms. Shelves of books and the owners' artworks make the place their own. Decorative touches come from natural objects like pebbles, driftwood, and shells.

Is this the perfect haven? "Sometimes we think it might be fun to have all this in a warmer climate, but then we wouldn't be as we are, only an hour away from our permanent home, and it is the changing weather conditions and the joy of the unexpected that we love. In truth we are quite besotted with our little hideaway!"

The owners spend up to three months at a time at their period beach hut: "We try to get here for most of the summer, and every weekend—even in winter when we have to brave the elements to do so." Mod cons extend to an ancient Baby Belling stove, a hip bathtub that "takes an age to fill" and oil-filled radiators. "Lots of blankets and thick comforters keep us warm in winter."

air

why air?

Of the four elements, air is perhaps the most mysterious. It envelops us, and we depend on it for life itself, but we cannot see it. Instead we rely on all our other senses to experience it. Our sense of smell is a powerful tool in our appreciation of air, and can trigger memories and emotions with remarkable accuracy. We smell warm, summer days in meadow grass and the metallic warning of rain to come. Closely linked is taste, as many flavours wouldn't be recognizable without the benefit of smell. For instance, the salty flavor of the air tells us instantly that we are by the ocean.

We hear air, too, in its different strengths and forms, through the whisper of wind through trees and the force of gales rattling windows in their frames. In urban areas we are bombarded by a continuous barrage of noise, and although we are able to filter out unwanted interference to some extent, its harm is not mitigated. So havens are associated with "peace and quiet"—but never silence. No matter how far from busy roads we take ourselves, we find nature's background noises—the hum of insects, the roll of waves, and the whistle of the wind. Yet, unlike stress-inducing man-made noises, they are a comfort and, rather like a lullaby, we can come to depend on them to soothe us into sleep.

"Go outdoors and get some fresh air" is a phrase we all remember from childhood. Experiencing this element is about being outside. Here, we actually touch the clean, fresh air—as refreshing and invigorating as a cold shower on a humid day. Eating, bathing, showering, and sleeping all take on a new dimension with the absence of a roof. One of these havens boasts an outdoor shower on a bridgelike structure that shoots out into the depths of the wild surrounds. At another, the owner swims in a pond he has dug himself and drinks "sundowners" surrounded by a panoramic view.

soothing, boundless
changing, elusive
swirling, soft
lofty, blowing
whispering
caressing, breathing
awakening
moving, fresh

textures, colors, patinas
up in the air

Air itself is clear, yet we need only look up at the dome of the sky that stretches from horizon to horizon to witness its myriad colors.

As a rule, air molecules scatter blue light more than any other color, which is why the sky is generally blue. The shade of blue will vary depending on other factors. Above the ocean, droplets of water suspended in the air scatter white light creating a pale blue sky; the dry air above the desert is purer, resulting in a deep blue sky. By contrast, the blue tone of the sky over our cities fades away in the haze of pollution.

The rainbow is perhaps the most wondrous display of color in the air. According to Greek mythology, it was the route between heaven and earth taken by Iris, a messenger of the gods. For the Shoshone tribe, it was a giant serpent that rubbed its back against a layer of ice that enclosed the sky. Mankind has always looked to the heavens for divine inspiration. And, just as plants grow up reaching into the sky for sunlight, so we are often drawn to experience the purity of air by climbing up high. Mountain retreats have long been renowned for their therapeutic properties. The owner of a treehouse hideaway describes the feeling he gets up in the treetops as one of escape and of rising above his everyday concerns. Here, among the fresh green growth of the leaves, air feels almost tangible as it brushes past, weightless, never still; always whirling, dancing, and invisibly caressing, air provides vital movement and levity. Air's colors are the fresh blues of a clear sky, the young greens of alpine forests; its textures are a cool breeze against our skin, the damp chill of a frosty morning. "Sharp and crisp" is how the owner of a Scottish hillside hideaway describes this element at its best.

apple, pistachio
chlorophyll
vision, grass
fresh, gauzy
sunshine, radiant
glossy, stippled

foliage, emerald
treetops

decorate your space with
air in mind

Fresh air is good for us. A cool wind revitalizes our spirits and refreshes our senses. It, quite literally, blows away the cobwebs. Houses need fresh air just as we do, so try to keep air on the move. Ceiling fans and air-conditioning units have their place, but natural ventilation is better for us. If possible, a building should be positioned so a breeze can circulate through all the rooms, because this keeps them fresh and alive, and, of equal importance, pleasantly cool during warm months. Note the prevailing direction of the wind throughout the year and plan the position of windows and doors accordingly. Old-fashioned beaded curtains at doorways allow air into a building while maintaining privacy; fine-gauge screens have the same function, with the added advantage of keeping insects and other unwelcome intruders out.

Endeavor to remove any barriers to seamless inside—outside living. French doors, stable doors, large picture windows, and the like create a visual and physical link between inside and outside spaces that positively encourages outdoor living. Seize every opportunity to eat outside—breakfast, lunch, and supper—it is one of the great pleasures of life. And rediscover the clothesline: laundry smells so much better dried in the open air. Hanging sheets outside (aromatic bushes like lavender were traditionally employed as drying lines) keeps them pristine and smelling fresh.

For your interiors, avoid heavy or dark materials and elaborately styled furnishings that will only weigh a room down. Pale colors and clean lines have the opposite effect. For windows, use ethereal, transparent fabrics like voile (which are easily washable, too) and discrete blinds or shades to create a fresh, unfussy look that maximizes the light and the feeling of space.

For floors and walls, space-enhancing colors like white and the palest blues and greens suggest airiness. Applying finishes with a sheen will again give an appearance of greater space by reflecting yet more light. Another practical step is to minimize the amount of furniture and clutter you have around you, since this will dramatically open up your home-away-from-home.

SPRUCE-TOP
TREEHOUSE

It's a happy coincidence that the owner of this haven should be a psychotherapist, for the desire to be alone, in a childlike den high up in the treetops raises interesting questions about the human psyche. What might prompt a grown-up to seek refuge in the treetops? The forest-dwelling ape languishing in our genetic make-up perhaps?

The owner's "personal-professional view" proves to be far more sophisticated: "Being up in the air, gives a feeling not just of escape but of 'rising above' other concerns," he says. "There are childhood connections, too: of climbing trees and building swings and dens in the branches, as well as perhaps associations with birds, flying, and *Peter Pan*. It also offers, quite literally, a different perspective on life."

Built as "a tranquil place to enjoy nature and the beautiful views and, more practically, to be an extra spare room for guests," the treehouse is strung between two Norway spruces over-looking a valley. It is close enough to the owner's cottage for electricity to be connected, but is so different from life on the ground as to instill the feeling of being, as he says, "far away from everything." One advantage of being so near the cottage is that cooking and washing can be taken care of back at base. However, the climb up has prompted the inclusion of an electric kettle and coffee maker. Most of the owner's leisure time is spent writing in the treehouse, and because it is heated—with an electric radiator—it can be used all year round.

"It really comes into its own in the summer though, when the French doors can be left open. It's ideal to sit out on the south-facing deck on lazy days, sunbathing with friends or reading." The treehouse is positioned so the deck area gets full sun, while the rest remains shaded by branches. "Being up there overlooking pasture, river, and woodland is very calming—particularly if the treehouse is swaying in a gentle breeze. And it adds another dimension to be on the same level as birds when they fly by."

The supporting frame of the treehouse is green oak, attached to the tree using harmless stainless-steel bolts. Cross beams are designed to slide on metal plates so the house moves with the tree. For the same reason, the windows are mounted in their frames with a flexible rubbery solution. Surprisingly, too much movement has only been a problem on one occasion, when the wind was so strong it caused the treehouse to judder "rather like turbulence in a plane."

Simple materials—pine decking, a blockboard floor, plywood panels— and a sparsity of creature comforts lend a monastic air—the view is the decoration—an impression enhanced by the Gothic-shaped windows, which are actually rectangular panes overlaid with narrow beading.

The treehouse is simply decorated inside. The dominant feature is the tree trunk growing through the structure, with its abundant cloak of ivy. White walls emphasize the generous light and contrast with the greenness all around.

Historically, humans have felt a need to be part of the cycles of nature. Being in this treehouse puts its owner even closer to the changes in the weather and the seasons. "In summer the valley is in full leaf, so everything seems near and lush, rather like a green 'sea' when the leaves and branches are swaying in the breeze. In fall mists shroud the valley floor, and the woods are a spectacular mix of russets, golds and reds—very much Keats' 'Season of mists and mellow fruitfulness.' In winter the landscape recedes, and the river can be clearly seen winding through the valley, while spring arrives gently with white blossom on the hawthorn and primroses in the woods."

eyrie

verdant

secret

lookout

camouflaged

elevated

panoramic

BACK TO
BASICS

"Being here is about experiencing the place itself rather than any material comforts; letting the surroundings dominate completely," says the architect and owner of this barn on a wooded hillside in Vermont.

Despite the clever architectural details (and the many examples of classic mid-century furniture), this haven is much more about getting back to basics than designer flourishes. There's no electricity, running water, or indoor plumbing, for instance—all water for cooking and washing is pumped by hand from the spring-fed pond. Yet for the owner, who, in his words, "works like a dog

This house in the woods, despite its designer flourishes, is an unsophisticated dwelling at heart. Indeed, the owner describes his haven as "just shelter in the landscape," while his wife sums it up as "glorified camping." Yet, despite these deprecatory statements, it is an approach they have been careful to preserve. It would be all to easy to make this get-away-from-it-all experience a mirror image of their home back in the city with all the mod cons we seemingly can't live without. But by resisting such luxuries—even down to plumbed-in conveniences—they are forced to "rough it." It is by removing ourselves from our cushioned existences that we are forced to experience the "cold turkey" of life at its very simplest.

felling trees and chopping firewood" whenever he goes there, the whole experience creates the perfect counterbalance to his loft-living existence in New York City.

Having acquired the 100-acre (40-hectare) site in Vermont several years ago, with the proviso that he wouldn't break it up, the owner unconventionally set about "inhabiting" the landscape by first creating a pond, then a meadow, and then a wood-fired hot tub, before finally starting on the barn or "hovel" as he calls it, many weekend work parties later. "Putting it simply, it's just a shelter in the landscape. For me the kick comes from editing that landscape, opening vistas, making the surroundings more airy. This is the way it would have been in the 1800s when this was a hillside farm with more meadow than trees, rather than the other way around as it was when we bought the place."

With a high peaked roof of corrugated metal, and 63 feet (20 meters) long by only 10 feet (3 meters) wide, the building draws its inspiration from indigenous agricultural buildings,

Space is a relative concept. Even large rooms can feel cramped if they are badly lit or filled with excess furniture and nicknacks. Positioned on a south-facing hillside to get morning and afternoon sun, the narrow barn is punctuated by a large picture window and ringed by translucent fiberglass slats that, with the sun beaming in, create the effect of being in a giant, airy light box united with the outside.

like the covered bridges and tobacco-drying barns of the region. However, for its ventilation, a "dog-trot" or open passageway that bisects the building, the architect–owner looked to the South. Thanks to this, even in the height of summer a cool breeze steals through the space. Its full of light, too. The slatted sides of the house appear open to the elements, but are actually interleaved with translucent fiberglass, which allows light in and out—to pretty effect at night—while being watertight and bugproof.

Jutting out into the valley on concrete pillars, 1,400 feet (425 meters) above sea level, the house was designed to take in the south-facing views of the surrounding mountains. "We get the best views and the best weather here. Although for me there's no such thing as unpleasant weather: listening to the rain falling, walking through the snow to get here, and heating the place with wood in the winter are all pleasurable aspects of being here—ways to connect back with the rituals of life—just as are physically working hard, carrying water, and chopping wood. My time here becomes a sort of

"Your mind is like a tepee. Leave the entrance flap open so the fresh air can enter and clear out the smoke of confusion."
Sioux saying

meditation through work." And yet there is fun, too, derived from the immediacy of nature and the elements: diving in the pond in summer; skating on it in winter; soaking in the hot tub outdoors; watching the visiting wildlife—deer, bears, wild ducks and turkeys, and the occasional moose— pass by; and shopping for berries, bread, flowers, and cheese from the organic farm stand miles back along the dirt track.

While his ability to rough it might be unusual, the owner's need for the haven as a balance to—but not a substitution for—his other, urban life is not. Asked could he imagine living here all year round, he answered succinctly, "Yes, but no," before expanding, "I'm very comfortable in the country, doing what I do there, but I enjoy it more when it is held in contrast to the city side of my life. I like the grit and push of New York, but I also like the absolute quiet of Vermont."

The upright stairs (above)— in true settler fashion—lead to a space-saving sleeping platform in the eaves. Great thought has gone into the placement of windows for the best light, views, and cooling breezes. The high-level window—matched by one at the opposite end of the barn—provides effective through-ventilation.

We are so used to the crowded lifestyle of towns and cities—the concrete jungles—that seclusion can come as something of a shock, albeit a liberating one. Here, the irregularity of the power supply and the threat of bears come hand-in-hand with the luxury of real privacy and the thrill of unrestricted freedom to do whatever the owners want whenever they want.

MOUNTAIN LIFE

So high is this escape—3,000 feet (1,000 meters) up in the Catskills—that, in the right weather, the owners can watch clouds moving through the valley below. "Being here is very much about experiencing the weather," they relate. "The entire south-facing wall of the house is glass, and looking across the valley—which runs east to west, so we have the sun all day—toward the hills and mountains opposite, there is a constantly changing wallpaper of light and sky. We can spend forever looking at the vastness of the hills."

A fashion stylist and journalist, both British and living in New York, the couple had been coming to the area for weekends on a regular basis. Exploring one day, they came along a dirt road that, after half a mile, led to the concrete foundations of a half-completed cabin deep in the woods. "The ruins were

set on a natural plateau, and as we came over the hill, the sudden expanse of space below was incredibly exciting. It felt like the south of France with the view and smell of wild thyme that forms a purple carpet all around."

With the help of an architect, they constructed a shedlike metal-and-wood building that partially used the existing foundations. "One of the things that really appealed to us about buying this plot was that we weren't eating up a piece of virgin land; the area had already been despoiled, and we like the fact that the architect's design has incorporated the modern ruin into the house. Being black, the building is a graphic shape that remains static while the surroundings change radically from

The hut is bisected by a long, bridgelike structure. At the rear (top left and above left) this bridge acts as a gentle pathway leading to the orchard and meadow, but at the front (top right) it is a metaphorical diving board—complete with outdoor shower—into the surrounding wilderness. The owners have deliberately kept furnishings functional—"when there's so much going on outside, you don't need decoration inside." For the same reason, utilitarian materials have been used throughout. Consequently, the hut was relatively cheap to build and yet, "the materials are true to themselves and take a lot of wear and tear."

privacy

open air

freedom

wilderness

seclusion

liberation

outdoors

sky

weather

Neutral tones create a low-key interior deliberately at odds with the vibrant, ever-changing view from the living room. The fireplace is a vital feature in winter when the power supply often fails, and the well freezes, so the owners have to resort to melting snow for water.

lush green through the sulfurous shades of fall to the total white-out of winter. The locals have nicknamed it 'the psycho chicken coop.'"

Low slung at the back, the hideaway appears settled into the landscape. Taller at the front where the wall of glass is, it appears to open up to the incredible vista, like a wide-angled lens capturing the view. Despite this, the couple's time there with their two small children is spent almost entirely outside. "We do capitalize on our seclusion. There are no visible neighbors, and even at night we cannot see the lights of any other properties. We bathe, cook, eat, shower, and sleep outside, in effect inverting our loft-living lifestyle in New York so here the outside becomes the inside. And even in winter we will use the hot tub just for the chance to be outdoors when it would be too cold to stand still otherwise. It's weird how the privacy affects you, you end up being quite reckless and uninhibited!"

Many of us are weighed down by the clutter of our lives, and it is only by going outdoors that we free ourselves. This couple love the outdoors with a passion—"Who isn't a nature lover?" they ask incredulously. Both brought up in the countryside, they relish the opportunity their 23 acres (10 hectares) afford their own family to create time to think and to experience the simple freedom to wander at will, free of crowds, traffic, and danger. "Just being able to let the children play outside in the open air is a luxury. It's a haven for them as much as it is for us."

The plywood ceiling adds warmth and exaggerates the feeling of coziness in the attic bedroom (this page). An "in-house wood-shop" supplied most of the pared-down furniture, including the beds and kitchen. "Building things for ourselves is extra therapy," say the owners.

The 1908 passenger carriage (Third Class) was rescued four years ago from a neighbor's yard where it had languished for some 50 years. The wonderfully distressed red paintwork on one side of the wagon has not been retained for its sense of character—"If it's left like that, the wood will only deteriorate!"—but merely indicates a work in progress.

RAILROAD
ESCAPE

As this old railroad wagon—now at rest high on a blustery Scottish hillside—proves, the perfect hideaway need be neither expensive nor far from home. Pragmatically positioned only two minutes' walk from the owner's farmhouse, it is, as he says, "just far enough to be out of hearing of the telephone."

Something of an amateur landscape architect, he has brought all four natural elements to bear in the location he chose for the carriage. Sited in a 10-acre (4-hectare) field beneath a typically windswept Scottish mountain, the wagon has magnificent panoramic views across the hillside to the north. The owner has dug a 6-foot (2-meter) deep pond, fed by a "burn," or stream, which he uses for daily swims. And he has planted

The paint colors chosen for the exterior and interior echo the natural surroundings—the soft greens of the grass and trees, and the vivid blues of the pond and sky. Perhaps for the same reason, they seem appropriately Scottish colors such as you might find in a traditional plaid tartan. The roof is coated annually with bitumen.

an 8-acre (3-hectare) native broadleaf wood nearby with wild cherry, rowan, hazel, birch, and elder, and some Scots pine and larch for winter color.

Although designated the "summerhouse," the wagon is in use year-round—part cozy nest, part sophisticated "beach hut" by the pond. In winter, the owner enjoys the effect of cocooning himself in a space smaller than his home. "When my house is too cold, I often go down to the wagon, light the wood stove, and enjoy a good read away from it all."

This owner has done all the work himself, engendering the feeling of a truly personal space and giving him a sense of "contributing to and preserving a piece of heritage." Like many of the owners of the hideaways in this book, his relationship with his haven is rather like that of a doting parent with a child. It demonstrates how important it is for us to make room for the things that have meaning to us, and

"Happy the man whose wish and care, A few paternal acres bound, Content to breathe his native air, In his own ground." Alexander Pope

Completely exposed on a hillside, the views from the wagon are far-ranging; "There's masses of sky," is how the owner puts it. Original fixtures add to the wonderful sense of character and history, and a collection of antique glass bottles plays with the generous light in the sunroom.

us alone. This doesn't have to be a perfect interior—more often, it is a collection of furnishings and accessories cobbled together from the things that we love.

"This is a place for 100 percent relaxation. There are no negative aspects to it," he maintains. "I even enjoy the changing weather, including heavy rain, when I'm in the wagon protected from it all. The lack of luxuries and return to simplicity are very much a positive aspect. I relax as soon as I close the door behind me—the 'clunk' sound takes me back 45 years to when I used to travel in similar cars pulled by steam locomotives. The nostalgia for those days helps me relax. I think I could very easily live there all year round—it's a nice thought—and perhaps once I've built my privy—American backwoods style—I will. It has all that I need."

fire

why fire?

Fire encompasses heat and light, and through the process of destruction, it begins the cycle of renewal. It embraces the colors of creativity, joy, and passion, and is synonymous with the sun—worshipped, above all else, by ancient civilizations.

We need fire to illuminate our world. Be it the glow of the sun, the flicker of a candle, or the slow burn of an electric bulb, the light fire gives out is essential if we are to see. "Light is so important to us," writes scientist Peter Ensminger, noting that our eyes have been called "the great monopolists of our senses." "A single glance instantly gives us information about our surroundings that is much more sophisticated than that from our other senses." Likewise, without light, there would be no color. The sun's white light contains every color of the rainbow, and as pigments absorb some of those rays and reflect others, so objects take on the reflected colors.

In addition to its light-giving properties, fire is also hot and dry. It bakes the earth in the desert; it burns up the moisture in logs as they crackle and spit in the hearth. Warm spaces and sunny days are synonymous with happy times, and these havens include an Airstream getaway in which the owners find peace under scorching desert skies; there is also a remote Scandinavian retreat that makes the most of every available ray, be it the dwindling sunlight or the glow of candlelight.

We are also compulsively drawn to the warmth and flickering flames of a real fire, exhibiting the kind of wonder and reverence that our hairier ancestors must have shown when they first learned to harness fire's power and, perhaps, took the primary steps toward creating and enjoying the concept of a home. In fact, a steadfast faith in the beauty and appeal of a real fire caused one owner here to design his fireplace first and then to build a barn around it. To twist an old homily, "Home is where the hearth is."

energizing
crackling, comforting
illuminating
warming, bright
flickering
intimate, cozy

textures, colors, patinas
from the fire

Fire takes on many forms, and the color of light emitted indicates the ferociousness with which an object is burning. Red, the color of cooling lava, is the coldest color of heat, followed by orange-yellow, the color of a candle flame, right through to white, the color of the surface of the sun.

As anyone who has stared into the embers of a fire will know, these shades can coexist, merging and mutating, reflecting the ever-changing presence of carbon and oxygen. Watching fire is to witness transformation.

These are the colors that speed the heart, incite passions, and stimulate the brain. Look at how the color of flames in a hearth merges with the russet tones of logs and the silver of ash. Admire a rosy-fingered dawn and absorb its mix of pale raspberry and frosty blue. Or pick up a pomegranate and note how the reds and yellows merge. The therapeutic use of color has been popular of late, but the trick to be learned is discovering which colors your body needs.

Fire encompasses extremes—scorching, blinding, burning—yet it is also homey and comforting. It is elusive, magical, uncontainable. Too hot to touch, we can only feel its effects and wonder at its power. We can sense it by the warmth penetrating our bodies sitting next to the fireside, by the heat of the sun on our skin; we can feel hot dry sand beneath our feet, and run our fingers over cracked earth that has been baked in the desert.

scarlet, emotive
intoxicating
deserts, black
patterned
embers, burned
white hot, blood red
glowing, hot

decorate your space with
fire in mind

Even today, when clean, unobtrusive, underfloor heating is all the rage, a generous fireplace will always form the focus of a room, promising coziness and refuge. Whatever the style of your decor, don't be afraid to sacrifice space to a real fire. The rewards are multiple, and you will wonder how you could have contemplated life without one.

The colors of fire are intense and advancing—visually, they leap toward you—and used en masse can easily overpower a room, reducing the appearance of space. Highly symbolic, the fiery shades can dramatically alter our moods and feelings: red is the color of physical drive; pink is calming; orange is the color of joy and dance, while yellow is intellectually stimulating and optimistic. Think how the room you are decorating will be used and choose your colur palette accordingly. White can also be the color of fire, but makes a cooling, contrasting counterpoint to the stronger tones, and lifts a space where light is at a premium.

It takes a courageous decorator to use the colors of fire across a whole room scheme, but the effects can be dramatic. Mix several fiery shades together to give interest and to relieve the intensity. Employed as accent colors against a neutral, earthy, or cool background, however, these shades add subtle warmth and movement, making us feel cosseted. Warmth in a room also comes from the textures we employ. A deep sheepskin rug, tactile fabrics like chenilles, velvets, luxurious woolens, and more minimalist materials such as suede can add to the nesting effect.

Masses of light is top of the modern homeowner's wish list. But too many windows can actually cause problems. Our forebears in climates with cold winters knew not to put windows on the north-facing side of a building and to keep other windows small, so reducing the amount of heat lost. In climates with hot summers windows should also be small, or shaded with overhanging eaves and shutters to keep the interior cool.

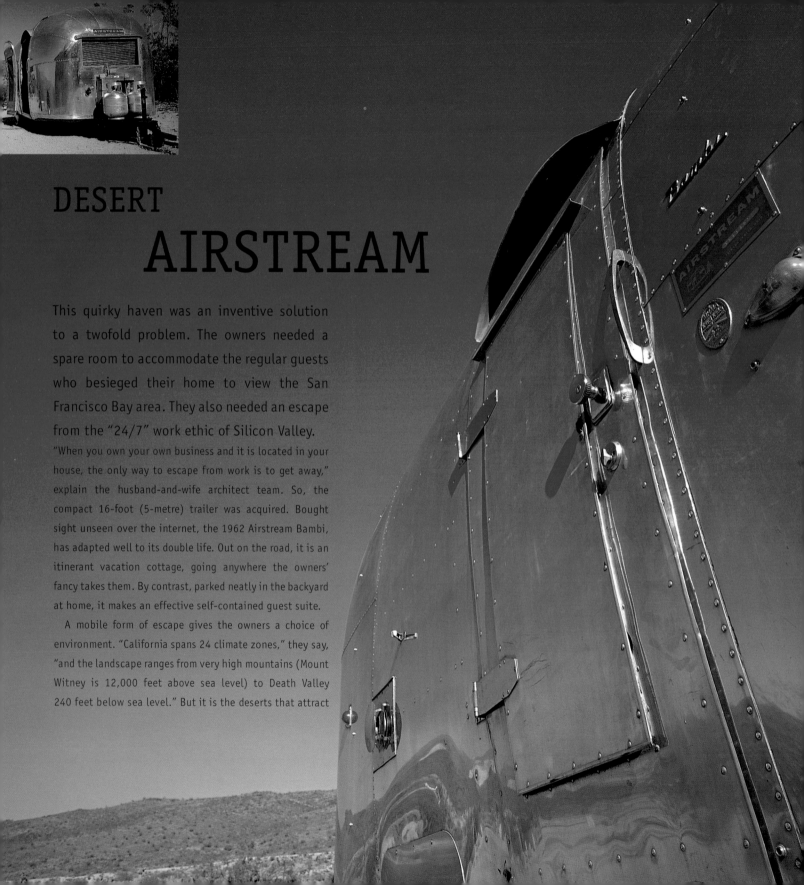

DESERT
AIRSTREAM

This quirky haven was an inventive solution to a twofold problem. The owners needed a spare room to accommodate the regular guests who besieged their home to view the San Francisco Bay area. They also needed an escape from the "24/7" work ethic of Silicon Valley.

"When you own your own business and it is located in your house, the only way to escape from work is to get away," explain the husband-and-wife architect team. So, the compact 16-foot (5-metre) trailer was acquired. Bought sight unseen over the internet, the 1962 Airstream Bambi, has adapted well to its double life. Out on the road, it is an itinerant vacation cottage, going anywhere the owners' fancy takes them. By contrast, parked neatly in the backyard at home, it makes an effective self-contained guest suite.

A mobile form of escape gives the owners a choice of environment. "California spans 24 climate zones," they say, "and the landscape ranges from very high mountains (Mount Witney is 12,000 feet above sea level) to Death Valley 240 feet below sea level." But it is the deserts that attract

the Airstream's owners. "The desert climate is by definition harsh and the landscape is made even more dramatic in the winter when the sun is low in the sky. Desert winter nights can be 14 hours long below freezing, with winds gusting up to 50 miles an hour. But Bambi tempers any weather conditions."

The owners have spent, on average, nearly a month each year in Bambi, exploring the many possibilities of living close to nature. "It's beyond the imagination; the mix of elements is inexhaustible and unpredictable. For us, where elements clash in nature make the best scenery, for instance an oasis in a desert, or a place where mountains meet the sea." The Airstream itself is perhaps a perfect example of this clash of extremes, forming a striking contrast between its lustrous, man-made form and the parched landscape of the desert.

The owners take Bambi—the smallest self-contained model of Airstream built—to places which are too remote to have lodgings or where development is not allowed, such as in National Parks. So the fact that it is entirely self-supporting — there is a gas stove, refrigerator, and hot and cold running water—is ideal. But it is a very pared-down lifestyle, not unlike camping: "When you are independent of the utility grid, you become acutely aware of every drop of water and every watt of electricity you use as well as the waste stream you produce and must deal with," say the owners. Its compact size encourages outdoor living, as do the empty acres of desert at their disposal.

The trailer required extensive restoration. Nearly 30 pounds (15 kg) of paint was stripped off the aluminum interior, and the original heavy enameled steel stove and sink were replaced with lightweight stainless-steel versions to help with fuel efficiency. Low-wattage light fixtures replaced inefficient steel-and-plastic versions. The owners also replaced a sandwich of vinyl flooring, particleboard, and linoleum with two-colored stripes of a Portuguese cork that is naturally occurring and renewable, "and lighter than any other flooring." The stripes help to counteract the narrowness of the space. Where the original fixtures couldn't be bettered, they have been retained. The original 38-year-old propane refrigerator (no CFCs) still

The Airstream's lightweight, aircraft-type construction inspired an "eco-restoration." Fixtures were assessed in terms of weight (for fuel-saving haulage) and eco-friendliness. For instance, veneered cabinets were rebuilt using aluminum, which is light and avoided the need for petrochemical finishes.

"In the desert, pure air and solitude compensate for want of moisture and fertility."
Henry David Thoreau

When the owner picked up the Airstream, "it had all the aesthetic charm of a roadside men's room." Today, it gleams inside and out. Cleverly planned, the compact interior adapts from daytime to bedtime with ease—the table folds away and the sofas transform into beds.

works, as do the propane space heater and the hot-water heater. And the tiny shower and toilet room remains unchanged—"the original Italian hand-held shower works better than any shower fixture in our house."

In the process of restoring the trailer's "romance of the road" character, the couple have collected aluminum artefacts—cookbook, trash can, ice chest, Ball-B-Q, and luggage—dating from the 1930 to 1970s, largely sourced over the internet. Retro fabrics also suit the vehicle's 1960s design and its "days gone by" atmosphere. But perhaps what most characterizes the decor are the ever-changing arrangements of leaves, sticks, colored sand, and rocks from the owners' latest visit to the desert.

HOMESTEAD
HEARTHSIDE

"I've always been fascinated by fire, so the idea of capturing fire in a vast opening where the focus of the room would be on the flames themselves ... was particularly appealing."

The fireplace built by the owner-architect of this snug Connecticut retreat, using huge rocks pulled from the surrounding land, is monolithic in scale and design. Lichen still grips the stones, and on a winter's night, it's not too fanciful to describe the effect as prehistoric and cavelike. "We burn fires every night from late fall through winter and use

The first building on the site was a simple wood-frame house. Later the small house was extended. Outbuildings followed (opposite), then the retreat, all arranged around a "green" in old New England style, interspersed with oaks and maples. "I wanted the buildings to be in scale and harmony with the landscape and to have a sense of permanence; to look as though they had always been there," says the owner.

"You are a
king by your
own fireside,
as much as
any monarch
in his throne."
Miguel de
Cervantes

candlelight, too, as it gives a wonderful glow. Such simple pleasures can be easily overlooked when people get caught up in their complicated worlds."

Having lived in towns and cities, the owner relishes his new way of life. "At night I return from the city and like the fact that I can hear nothing of the outside world. It's always a pleasure to come home. This is a wonderfully peaceful place where you're constantly conscious of changes in the weather and the progress of the seasons—each has a distinct character, though the color of the fall has to make it the greatest season. From October onwards the forest looks as though it is on fire with reds, oranges, and yellows. And there's a crispness to the air, a feeling of things changing and getting ready for winter and, of course, we can start stacking wood and laying fires. It's a very special spot; as havens go, this isn't bad at all."

The retreat is essentially one large room anchored by an expanse of glass at one end and the monumental fireplace at the other. Tucked behind the fire is a bedroom, kept ready for visits by the extended family. The owners also use the space as a retreat from the main house: "a haven within a haven, we go there to read and relax, and often cook simple suppers in the fireplace."

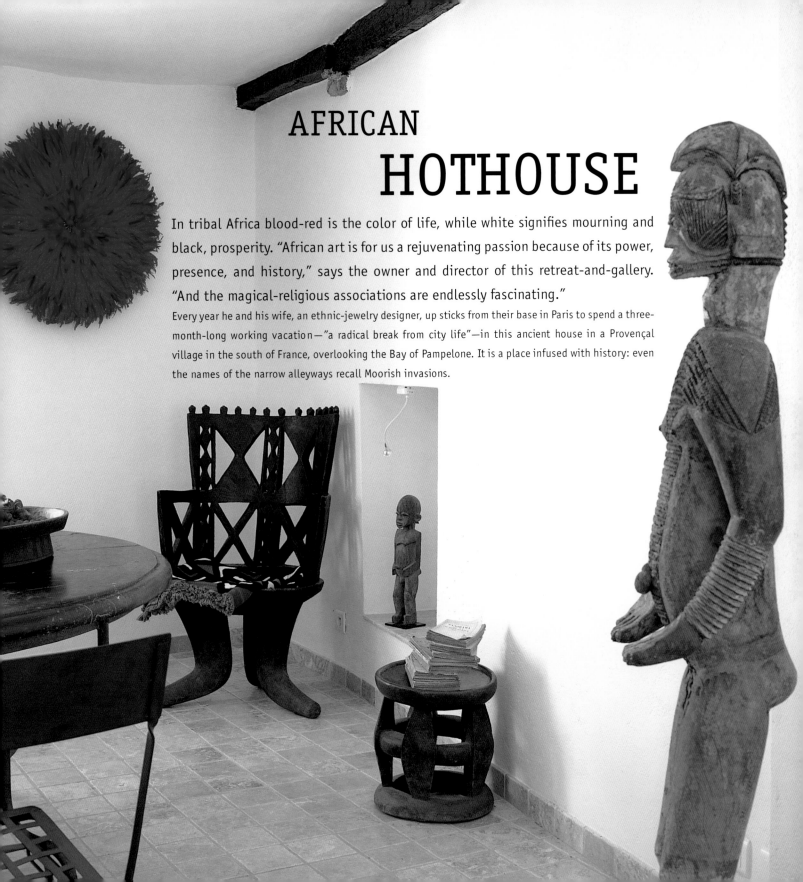

AFRICAN
HOTHOUSE

In tribal Africa blood-red is the color of life, while white signifies mourning and black, prosperity. "African art is for us a rejuvenating passion because of its power, presence, and history," says the owner and director of this retreat-and-gallery. "And the magical-religious associations are endlessly fascinating."

Every year he and his wife, an ethnic-jewelry designer, up sticks from their base in Paris to spend a three-month-long working vacation—"a radical break from city life"—in this ancient house in a Provençal village in the south of France, overlooking the Bay of Pampelone. It is a place infused with history: even the names of the narrow alleyways recall Moorish invasions.

Fiery colors don't need to be used en masse to be effective. Here, isolated, eye-catching splashes of ruby red bring glamour and drama to the otherwise understated rooms. The sculptural, dark-wood furniture — "the color of burnt bread," as the owner describes it—is mainly Asian. Although created in a different continent from its final resting place, the hand-made, timeworn quality of the pieces sits well with the simple Provençal cottage and its clay tiles and ancient gnarled beams.

Living with heat has its own set of problems; here it is solved by thick solid walls and traditional shutters. Employed throughout the Mediterranean countries to let air circulate while keeping out the sun's glare, the shutters keep the house cool, even in summer when the region enjoys relentless sunshine. Inside, the once-cramped interior has been opened up and doors done away with to increase the sense of space dramatically. With the shutters thrown open, light courses through, bouncing off uniformly white walls which act as a stark backdrop to the owner's collection of tribal sculptures and textiles and Asian furniture.

In winter, fires are lit in the old fireplace made of traditional, baked clay tiles. "The weather is mild in the Mediterranean all year round, but we light a fire to create a cozy atmosphere and keep out the damp," relates the owner, "We also light lots of brightly colored scented candles to lift the room and create a relaxing atmosphere."

Outside, the garden is planted with pungent herbs, including thyme, basil, and rosemary, and scented plants such as lavender. They release their aroma in the dry heat to fill the air with a relaxing cocktail of aromatherapy.

tribal

powerful

symbolic

bold

jewel

bright

contrasting

NORTHERN
LIGHTS

In Sweden, people have had to learn to value the soft beauty and healing effects of natural light, as the days are brutally short from mid-autumn through to early spring.

The mid-point of the long, dark winter season—the longest night of the year—is marked by the Festival of Light, St. Lucia's Day in December, when celebrations center around the lighting of many candles. Candlelight is an important feature at this converted distillery on a farm in southern Sweden. "While we do have electric light, we rarely use it; instead we burn a large number of candles," say the owners. "Artificial light is so strong and cold we prefer the warmth and glow—and the atmosphere of centuries long lost—that candlelight gives."

airy
reflective
pale
iridescent
gleaming
shadowy
romantic

The owners are mindful, though, of the destructive powers of naked flames and open fires. The distillery, being stone, is all that remains of the original period farm buildings which a fire destroyed just 30 years ago. The outbuildings have since been rebuilt in the Scandinavian softwood traditionally used as a building material.

The farmstead is some distance from the nearest village, which gives it a feeling of isolation that particularly appealed to the owners. "For us there is a special feeling that comes from living in the country and being alone. The peace enhances our closeness to the elements, and we have the knowledge that nature is always just around the corner for us to enjoy."

In Scandinavia, softwood is commonly used for building and furniture, so, over the years, paint finishes have been developed to protect it and to disguise its unsophisticated appearance. Rich warm colors like deep blue or red are used to merge buildings' exteriors with the landscape.

The romantic, seductive effect of candlelight has become something of a cliché, but—perhaps because we are so used to the all-encompassing reach of electric light—we easily forget what pleasure there is to be had in the patchwork of shadow and glow found in a room lit only by candle- and firelight. We need shadows not just for intimacy but for relaxation and meditation. Where electric light is necessary, restrict its dominance by using task lighting designed specifically for the job in hand.

The owners are devotees of 18th- and 19th-century traditional Swedish style—Gustavian in particular—and are also antique dealers. Their antique store is on the ground floor, while their living space on the second floor benefits from the extra light that being up in the air affords.

The desire to exploit natural light is not a purely aesthetic one. Through the winter months, when the sun never rises above the surrounding treetops, spirits can be dimmed along with the sun's rays. The inhabitants of this hideaway recognize this fact and the corresponding need for a regular dose, quite literally, of sunlight to maintain health and happiness. Therefore, as is traditional in

Swedish interiors, the layout of the converted distillery is designed and decorated with two conflicting aims in mind: being warm and cozy during the long winters while maximizing every last drop of precious daylight.

Heat-retaining small windows are offset by pale walls throughout the interior—painted with a traditional soft off-white distemper that gently scatters and reflects the light and complements the light-enhancing whites and gray-blues used on the painted furniture. Internal doors are "glazed" with fine-mesh screen that allows the hazy passage of light between rooms, and at the windows there are simple, traditional rolled shades, rather than obstructive curtains.

The owners' preference for firelight and candlelight as natural mood lighting immediately creates a warm ambience through the constantly flickering flames and shadows and the associated aromas of beeswax and pinewood that fill the house. The placing of mirrors, sconces, and chandeliers combines with the soft light and magnifies it through reflection. It's an old device that originates in earlier centuries when candles were a luxury.

To fuel their passion for firelight, the owners spend many of the long daylight hours of summer collecting and chopping firewood in the surrounding forests, which they leave to dry ready for the winter months.

Gustavian style is both classical and minimalist. Furnishings are understated and sparsely arranged—a sense of space, freedom of movement, and views between rooms are considered essential to creating an airy, light feel. Decoration comes in the form of elegant, light-enhancing accessories such as silver candlesticks and glassware.

why earth?

We talk of "Mother Earth," "going to earth," "coming down to earth." Put simply, earth is home, and we have a bond to the ground beneath our feet that cannot be broken.

Yet we take earth for granted. The Vietnamese Buddhist monk Thich Nhat Hanh, wrote, "The real miracle is not to walk either on water or in thin air, but to walk on earth." Experiencing the element of earth is about experiencing nature. But it is only when we are released from modern pressures, fully immersed in the natural world, that we see its abundant beauty with fresh eyes.

Even confirmed city dwellers have a deep-seated affinity to the earth. You need only think of the treatments on offer at health spas in every metropolis to be reminded of our sensual and spiritual relationship with this element. We smear our bodies in mineral-rich mud; have hot rocks placed on our aching backs; and immerse ourselves in darkened tanks of salt-choked water. It is hardly surprising, then, that so many of us seek a haven where we can reconnect with the earth.

If you are building your haven from scratch, the siting of the dwelling in the surrounding landscape—its connection with the earth—should be as important, if not more so, than the design of the structure itself. *Shelter* (the authoritative work on the building of rudimentary huts and hideaways) offers the following inspirational advice. "Before you decide on a design or materials, you should consider the site: how you will be affected by sun, wind, rain, summer and winter climate, roads, outlook, trees, neighbors, cars, birds ... watch the angle of the sun change throughout the year, learn where the winter storms come from, and figure how to have the morning sun at your breakfast table."

enduring, growth
reassuring
fruitful, home
safety, fertile
bountiful
stability, nurturing
grounding

textures, colors, patinas
in the earth

Earth is the color and texture of stone, soil, straw, wood, bark, leather, and the autumn harvest. Earth is nature's old age; vibrant flowers that are spent and turned to seed heads; green leaves that have fallen and crumbled to humus on the forest floor. Earth encourages us to connect with our environment; it is a tactile element—who hasn't run their fingers through sand, crumbled loamy soil, or stroked the knotted whorls on a tree branch?

The colors of earth are reassuring, warm and inviting, the colors of commitment. They immediately make us feel at home, perhaps because they remind us of nature. And what would our homes be like without earth's rich bounty? Without stone for walls and floors, clay for bricks, pottery, and tiles, and the different woods for furniture and accessories?

Earth comprises a wide and harmonious palette, one that has been relied on by painters for centuries—think of the mineral pigments of sienna, ocher, umber—a fact recognized by the naming of a mineral-rich region of Death Valley National Park, California, Artist's Palette. And yet many of these colors are the result of compounds formed from a small group of metals—iron, copper, and manganese, among them. Indeed, iron oxide alone can be red (as in rust), green, pink, or yellow.

Earth's many elements have a timeless beauty and character that improves with age and use. Mix any of these hues and textures together, in any combination, and they will work. They have a sympathy with one another that makes them somehow "right."

hazelnut, soil
parchment
bark, nutmeg
pelt, stone
pecan, autumn
ocher, peat
cinnamon
clay, putty
sienna, iron
cocoa, umber

decorate your space with
earth in mind

Although essentially grounding, the browns of the earth can magically metamorphose depending on how they are used.

Browns are brought alive by warm, fiery colors like orange and red—think of the colors of a New England fall. Teamed with white and cream, browns look resolutely chic and modern. Partnered with powder blue or celadon green, they take on a relaxed, sophisticated air. For textural interest, use natural textiles like linen and hemp, and flooring like sisal, rush, and seagrass, all of which are incredibly hard-wearing, and whose irregular tones add subtle movement.

Investing in traditional handcrafted items—a capacious farmhouse table, deftly woven rush matting—is money well spent. These designs have been tested over centuries, after all, and will be heirlooms for generations to come. So seek out craftspeople who keep traditional skills alive and commission items for your home instead of buying off the shelf. Not only will you have something unique, but you will be reassured that neither the planet nor the maker was exploited in its creation.

Natural colors have a character and subtlety that unites them. Investigate traditional pigments and mix your own paint and dye colors. Take inspiration for shades that sit well together from the natural world. Not only will your house be full of colors that sing out to you—in a way chemical colors can't touch—but you will be saving the environment from unnecessary pollution.

STRAWBALE
HOUSE

Set within a wooden framework, the bales were built up into walls like giant bricks and overlaid with traditional lime mortar. Unlike modern renders, lime breathes, allowing moisture to pass through. The mortar was dressed with a deep ocher distemper which sits well with the age-worn textures of the reclaimed door and windows and the soft red of the old clay brick.

There is fun in "playing house" in any ramshackle or rudimentary dwelling—the smaller the better. This is undoubtedly a throwback to childhood pleasures: camping on the lawn; building lookouts in trees; and constructing wigwams from furniture and blankets! The owner of this tiny dwelling was motivated to build her bolthole by "lack of privacy, stress, and a need to escape." Unusually, it was not city life she was escaping. Sharing her 80-room, 16th-century manor house with a furniture-making business, a college of residential craftspeople, and, for 7 months of the year, the general public, she felt an overriding urge "to find peace and calm, and to be at one

Despite the "man-made" environment, there is a feeling that nature envelops the little house entirely. "The vegetable patch is a tumbling confusion of untidy beauty," says the owner. "It's the total antithesis to the formal gardens of the manor house—with roses, buddleia, and clematis left to flower, and herbs all intermingled with the many vegetables such as yellow, purple, and green beans, unusual lettuces, and obscure tomatoes." Practically self-sufficient, she can make a wonderful meal within minutes of picking the ingredients.

with nature." The result is a very intimate and humble abode, completely at odds with her rather grand apartments back in the heritage house. "I wanted to remove myself from 'real' life, people, the telephone, and from sophistication. I had a yearning for the intimacy of a small space. Time spent in my hideaway is peaceful and productive. I write and garden and daydream—working through problems and gaining a sort of mental 'space.'"

An accomplished gardener, she felt a need to connect with the rhythms of nature and the earth, and was drawn to create her haven in the abandoned Victorian walled kitchen garden. "Although within the demesne of the big house, the location is utterly remote in terms of privacy. Most people looking in would have no idea that my hideaway existed. Even on entering the gardens, it is not immediately visible; a rose hedge, greenhouse and apple tree hide it from view."

The strawbale house was built in a corner of the garden against two of the old 15-foot (4.5-meter) high brick walls, by her eldest son and a carpenter friend. The

"Small rooms
or dwellings
discipline the
mind, large
ones weaken it."
Leonardo da Vinci

bales were built into a wooden framework—actually old show-jumping poles—and covered with traditional lime mortar. Contrary to the experience of the Three Little Pigs, strawbale buildings are not easily demolished, but are in fact known for their solidity. They are also supremely cheap to build, long lasting and environmentally friendly, because they use renewable, non-toxic, locally available materials and have excellent insulation properties.

"Bird life is wonderful here, varied and very tame. Wrens, fly catchers, robins, blackbirds, finches, nuthatches, and owls all visit. There are hedgehogs galore, and wild bees and hornets nest in the garden walls. One feels very close to the elements—yet able to be warm on bitter winter days, or cool on hot summer ones—the ever-changing view of the skies, clouds, sun, and moon becomes part of one's immediate consciousness. It would be nice to have far-reaching views, perhaps of the sea, and the opportunity to watch the sunset, but then I wouldn't have the feeling of privacy and seclusion that my walled garden offers."

The old south-facing brick walls were used by the manor's gardeners for their heat-retaining properties—espaliered fruit trees would have been tied to wires to luxuriate in their warmth. Coupled with the thick straw walls, they keep the space amazingly well insulated. Even in winter, the wood-burning stove (opposite) heats the room very quickly (once the stove has gone out, the warmth is retained for up to 24 hours), while in summer the deep veranda shades the windows from direct sunlight and the little house stays pleasantly cool. The makeshift outdoor kitchen (this page) boasts an old ceramic sink, cold running water, and a tiny Italian oven with a grill. Water for washing is heated on the stove.

CONVERTED
DAIRYHOUSE

Since ancient times, man has had a desire to leave his mark on the landscape. Yet for a domestic building to achieve longevity, it must work both physically with its environment and practically for its inhabitants.

Situated alongside a small working farm, nestling in a patchwork of fields, this house is molded by the gentle slope of the land. Despite the apparent starkness of its design, the relationship of the building to the landscape and its inhabitants' experience of their surroundings has been given great thought. On

The living room and eating space focus on the patchwork of sheep-filled fields that stretch across the valley. In an effort to be in sympathy with the landscape and existing agricultural buildings, the house was built with untreated materials like cedar, aluminum, and plywood so that, chameleonlike, they would weather quickly and blend in with the silvery-browns of the local limestone.

sympathetic

mellow

weathered

timeless

understated

secluded

natural

seamless

evolving

the upper level, the old dairy has been converted into three bedrooms and a bathroom. On the lower level, the rickety lean-to cowshed has been demolished and replaced with a resolutely modern building, housing the roomy living and eating spaces. The two levels are connected by a half flight of stairs so, the architects explain, "there is still the reassuring sensation of going up to bed."

Our sense of touch is what connects us to life. When we feel, we "see" with our bodies. Therefore, in creating a place to escape to, it is important to make it one that adds to your life in this very real, very tangible way. In this conversion, the space cleverly combines the coolness of textured stone underfoot and the patina of wood to echo the earthiness of the outside.

The space's ease within its rural environment is maintained with the help of rough-hewn ceramics, such as these handthrown pots (above). Here, even simple pleasures, like breakfast in bed or afternoon tea outdoors seem special.

SECRET
GARDEN

"I am not often willing to share my hidden corner of paradise," relates the owner of this rusticated hideaway. "In fact, I have shown it, with parsimony, to only a few friends and the people closest to me."

"My little garden acts as a retreat when I feel the need to get away from work and recover some peace of mind. The country air, musty smell of the earth, and cold water are, for me, the essence of closeness to nature, whose healing effect counterbalances the hectic, time-structured existence we are forced to live nowadays. Just to cut the grass, look at the flowers, sit in the sun on the bench gives me a sense of being far away 'from the madding crowd.' When the time comes to leave, my emotional batteries are recharged and I return full of optimism to tasks which previously seemed difficult to tackle."

Situated on the outskirts of a medieval Provençal village, the garden and *bastidon* (a tiny Provençal cottage) may be just minutes away from the owner's home, but the journey there—almost a trip back in time—and the garden's seclusion and simple character contrive to provide all that she requires from her haven. "From my house in the center of the village, I walk through a medieval stone gate, cross a street, and enter a

The owner has been careful not to alter the atmosphere of the *bastidon*, so the broken red floor tiles, the patina of the walls and woodwork, and the old tools—now used as decorative objects on the wall—remain, married with rickety chairs and unpretentious fabrics like soft voile and traditional Provençal prints.

small passage that takes me to the iron gate of the walled gardens surrounding the south side of the town, which are, for the main part, owned by very old ladies who grow vegetables and keep rabbits and chickens there for their families."

"The longer I stay here, the more I feel penetrated by a sensation of being part of a rural past with all that implies. My nostalgia for the past, 'La Vieille France,' with which I fell in love as a child, was what made me leave my native Germany and take French nationality. In fact, my attachment to the colors, textures, and smells of the seasons, the simplicity of the place, and the closeness of nature and the past have become an addiction, so much so that I am reluctant to travel elsewhere. It is only here that I truly feel at home."

warm

nurturing

earthy

sheltered

rustic

ancient

mysterious

nostalgic

sources and
contacts

FURNITURE AND ACCESSORIES

The Conran Shop
Bridgemarket
415 East 59th Street
New York, NY 10022
212-755-9079
www.conran.com

The Cotton Place
PO Box 59721
Dallas, TX 75229
800-451-8866

KB Cotton Pillows Inc.
PO Box 57
De Soto, TX 75123
800-544-3752
www.kbcottonpillows.com

Crate & Barrel
Flagship location:
646 N Michigan Avenue
Chicago, IL 60611
800-996-9960
www.crateandbarrel.com

IKEA
Flagship location:
1800 East McConnor Parkway
Schaumburg, IL 60173
www.ikea.com

Restoration Hardware
Flagship location:
935 Broadway
New York, NY 10011
212-260-9479
www.restorationhardware.com

Rising Star Futons
35 Bond Street
Bend, OR 97701
800-828-6711

Shaker Shops West
PO Box 487
Inverness, CA 94937
415-669-7256
www.shakershops.com

Sofa U Love
11948 San Vicente
Brentwood, CA 90049
310-207-2540

Williams-Sonoma
150 Post Street
San Francisco, CA 94108
415-362-6904
877-812-6235 for nearest store
www.williams-sonoma.com

Workshop Showcase
PO Box 500107
Austin, TX 78750
512-331-5470

Yield House
PO Box 2525
Conway, NH 03818-2525
800-258-4720

NATURAL FABRICS

Cotton Plus Limited
Route One, PO Box 120
O'Donnell, TX 79351
806-439-6646

Foxfibre Vreseis Ltd.
PO Box 87
Wickerburg, AZ 85358
502-684-7199
www.foxfibre.com/cotton

The Ohio Hempery
7002 State Route 329
Guysville, OH 45735
800-BUY-HEMP

FLOORING AND CARPETS

Hendricksen Natürlich
PO Box 1677
Sebastopol, CA 95473-1677
707-824-0914

Image Carpets
Highway 140, PO Box 5555
Armuchee, GA 30105
800-722-2504
www.imageind.com

Sustainable Lifestyles
PO Box 313
Excelsior, MN 55331
800-287-3144

World Fibre
PO Box 480805
Denver, CO 80248
303-628-2210

AIR FILTER SYSTEMS

Aireox Research Corp.
PO Box 8523
Riverside, CA 92515
909-689-2781

Airguard Industries Inc.
PO Box 32578
Louisville, KY 40232
302-969-2304
www.airguard.com

BUILDING MATERIALS

Building for Health Materials Center
PO Box 113
Carbondale, CO 81623
970-963-0437

Environmental Home Center
1724 4th Avenue
Seattle, WA 98134
800-281-9785

Faswall Concrete Systems
1676 Nixon Road
Augusta, GA 30906
706-793-8880

Structural Slate Company
222 E Main Street
Pen Argyl, PA 18072
610-863-4827

Terra Green Technologies
1650 Progress Drive
Richmond, IN 47374
317-935-4760

EARTH-BUILDING MATERIALS

Adobe Building Supply
5609 Alameda Place NE
Albuquerque, NM 87113
505-828-9800

Hans Sumpf Company Inc.
40101 Avenue 10
Madera, CA 93638
209-439-3214

TIMBER

Ecotimber International
1020 Heinz Avenue
Berkeley, CA 94710
510-549-3000

Goodwin Heart Pine Company
106 SW 109 Place
Micanopy, FL 32667
800-336-3118
www.heartpine.com

Woodworkers Source
5402 South 40th Street
Phoenix, AZ 85040
602-437-4415
www.woodworkersource.com

PAINT, FINISHES, AND SEALERS

**American Formulating &
Manufacturing (AFM)**
350 West Ash Street, Suite 700
San Diego, CA 92101
800-239-0321

Auro Organic Paints
Imported by Sinan Natural Building
Materials
PO Box 857
Davis, CA 95617-0857
916-753-3104
www.dcn.davis.ca.us/go/sinan

The Natural Choice ECO Design
1365 Rufina Circle
Santa Fe, NM 87505
505-438-3448

Wm Zinsser & Company Inc.
173 Belmont Drive
Somerset, NJ 08875
732-469-4367
www.zinsser.com

TIMBER FRAME HOMES

Pacific Post & Beam
PO Box 13708
San Luis Obispo, CA 93406
805-543-7565

Thistlewood Timber Frame Homes
RR #6, Markdale, ON NOC 1HO
Canada
519-986-3280
www.interlog.com/~thistle

KIT HOMES

Airstream Trailers
PO Box 629, 419 West Pike Street
Jackson Center, OH 45334
937-596-6111
www.airstream-rv.com

Deltec
604 College Street
Asheville, NC 28801
800-642-2508
www.deltechomes.com

Design Works Inc.
11 Hitching Post Road
Amherst, MA 01002
413-549-4763

Haiku Houses
Design Plaza
250 Newport Center Drive
Suite 200
Newport Beach, CA 92660
714-720-0499
www.tdmdesign.com/haiku/

Living Systems Group
PO Box 875
Rainier, WA 98576
800-820-1611

Pacific Yurts, Inc.
77456 Highway 99 South
Cottage Grove, OR 97424
800-944-0240
www.yurt.com

HEATING AND ENERGY CONSERVATION

Alternative Energy Systems
Alternative Energy Engineering
PO Box 339
Redway, CA 95560
800-800-0624

Backwoods Solar Electric Systems
8530 Rapid Lightening Creek Road
Sandpoint, ID 83864
208-263-4290

Kansas Wind Power
13569 214th Road
Holton, KS 66436
913-364-4407

Real Goods
555 Leslie Street
Ukiah, CA 95482
800-762-7325
www.realgoods.com

Solar Electric Specialties
PO Box 537
Willits, CA 95490
800-344-2003
www.solarelectric.com

Tulikivi US Inc.
PO Box 7825
Charlottesville, VA 22906-7825
www.tilikivi.com

Zomeworks Corporation
PO Box 25805
Albuquerque, NM 87125
www.zomeworks.com

INSULATION

Air Krete Palmer Industries
10611 Old Annapolis Road
Frederick, MD 21701
301-898-7848

Greenwood Cotton Insulation Products, Inc.
70 Manswell Court, Suite 100
Roswell, GA 30076
404-998-6888

International Cellulose Corp.
12315 Robin Boulevard
Houston, TX 77045
800-444-1252
www.spray-on.com

WATER FILTERS AND PURIFIERS

Ametek Plymouth Products Division
PO Box 1047
Sheboygan, WI 53082-1047
800-222-7558

General Ecology Inc.
151 Sheree Boulevard
Lionville, PA 19353
610-363-7900

Multi-Pure
21339 Nordhoff Street
Chatsworth, CA 91311
818-341-7577
www.multipure.com

The Pure Water Place Inc.
PO Box 6715
Longmont, CO 80501
303-776-0056

TESTING

National Testing Laboratories
6555 Wilson Mills Road, Suite 102
Cleveland, OH 44143
216-449-2525
www.watercheck.com

Radon Testing Corporation of America
2 Hayes Street
Elmsford, NY 10523
800-457-2366
www.rtca.com

GARDENING

Abundant Life Seed Foundation
PO Box 772
Port Townsend, WA 98368
www.abundantlifeseed.org

Biosphere 2 Center
Department of Education
PO Box 689
Oracle, AZ 85623
520-896-5075

Egogenesis Inc.
Box 1929, 3266 Yound Street
Toronto, ON M4N 3P6
Canada
416-489-7333

Seeds of Change
PO Box 15700
Santa Fe, NM 87506
505-983-8956

Smith & Hawken
117 East Strawberry Drive
Mill Valley, CA 94941
415-383-4415

MAGAZINES AND JOURNALS

Eco-Building Times
Northwest EcoBuilding Guild
217 9th Avenue North
Seattle, WA 98109
206-622-8350

Eco-Design Quarterly
PO Box 3981, Main Post Office
Vancouver, BC V6B 3Z4
Canada
604-738-9334

Environmental Building News
RR1, Box 161
Brattleboro, VT 05301
802-257-7300
www.ebuild.com

Fine Homebuilding
Taunton Press
63 South Main Street
PO Box 5506
Newtown, CT 06470
203-426-8171
www.taunton.com

Mother Earth News
49 East 21st Street, 11th floor
New York, NY 10010
212-260-7210
www.motherearthnews.com

Organic Gardening
Rodale Press
PO Box 7320
Red Oak, IA 51591-0302
www.rodalepress.com

Sustainable Living News
PO Box 45472
Seattle, WA 98145
206-323-6567

ORGANIZATIONS

American Council for an Energy-Efficient Economy
1001 Connecticut Avenue NW
Suite 801
Washington, DC 20036
202-429-8873
aceee.org

American Institute of Architects
1735 New York Avenue NW
Washington, DC 20006-5292
802-626-7300

American Society of Heating, Refrigeration and Air Conditioning Engineers Inc.
17191 Tullie Circle NE
Atlanta, GA 30329-3025
404-636-8400
www.ashrae.org

American Solar Energy Society
2400 Central Avenue, Suite G-1
Boulder, CO 80301
www.ases.org/solar

American Wind Energy Association
122 C Street NW, 4th floor
Washington, DC 20001
202-383-2500
www.econet.org/awea/

Architects Designers & Planners for Social Responsibility
65 Bleecker Street
New York, NY 10012
212-924-7893

Center for Resourceful Building Technology
PO Box 100
Missoula, MT 59806
406-549-7678

Eco-Home Network
4344 Russell Avenue
Los Angeles, CA 90027
213-662-5207

Energy Efficiency & Renewable Energy Clearinghouse (EREC)
PO Box 3048
Merrifield, VA 22116-0121
800-363-3732
www.eren.doe.gov

The Health House Institute
430 N Sewell Road
Bloomington, IN 47408
812-332-5073

National Fenestration Ratings Council
1300 Sprint Street
Suite 120
Silver Springs, MD 20910
301-589-6372

National Renewable Energy Laboratory
1617 Cole Boulevard
Golden, CO 80401
303-275-3000
www.nrel.gov

The Natural House Building Center
2300 West Alameda, #A5
Sante Fe, NM 87501
505-471-5314

Northeast Sustainable Energy Association
23 Ames Street
Greenfield, MA 01301
413-774-6051

Scientific Certification Systems
1939 Harrison Street, Suite 400
Oakland, CA 94612
510-832-1415
www.scs1.com

Shelter Institute
38 Center Street
Bath, ME 04530
207-442-7938
www.shelterinstitute.com

Straw Bale Association of Texas
3102 Breeze Terrace
Austin, TX 78722
512-499-0526
www.greenbuilder.com/sourcebook/
strawbale.html

Timber Framers Guild of North America
PO Box 1075
Bellingham, WA 98227-1075
360-733-4001
www.tfguild.org

The Water Quality Association
4151 Naperville Road
Lisle, IL 60532
708-505-0160

credits

ARCHITECTS AND DESIGNERS
WHOSE WORK IS FEATURED
IN THIS BOOK

Jonathan Adler
465 Broome Street
New York, NY 10013
Tel 212-941-8950
Pottery, lighting, and textiles
Pages 4–7, 16–17b, 18–23, 140c,
144

anderson architects
555 West 25th Street
New York, NY10001
Tel 212-620-0996
Fax 212-620-5299
info@andersonarch.com
www.andersonarch.com
Pages 2, 61al, 66–79, 139c, 144

**Simon Kimmins Design and Project
Control**
Tel +44 20-8314-1526
Pages 1, 62–65

**Interior designer Nicoletta
Marazza**
Tel +39 02760-14482
Pages 16–17a, 17ar, 34–39

M. J. Marcinik
Greenmeadow Architects
4046 Ben Lomond Drive
Palo Alto, CA 94306
Pages 88, 92b, 94–99

Marston Properties Ltd
1 Stephendale Road
London SW6 2LU
UK
Tel +44 20-7736-7133
Fax +44 20-7731-8412
ellie@marstonproperties.co.uk
Pages 118, 122bl, 123bl, 130–133,
139l

Schefer Design
David Schefer & Eve-Lynn
Schoenstein
41 Union Square West, No. 1427
New York, NY1003
Tel 212-691-9097
Fax 212-691-9520
Scheferdesign@mindspring.com
www.scheferdesign.com
Pages 4–7, 16–17b, 18–23, 140c,
144

Sergisson Bates
44 Newman Street
London W1P 3PA
UK
Tel +44 20-7255-1564
Fax +44 20-7636-5646
Pages 118, 122bl, 123bl, 130–133,
139l

Stenhuset Autilehandle
Bögerupsgård
24196 Stockamöllan
Skane, Sweden
Pages 3, 92a, 93bl, 108–115

Bernard M. Wharton
Shope Reno Wharton Associates
18 West Putnam Avenue
Greenwich, CT 06830
Tel 203-869-7250
srwol@aol.com
www.shoperenowharton.com
Pages 93ar&l, 100, 102–103

BIBLIOGRAPHY

Writing on Water, David Rosenberg
and Marta Ulvaeus. MIT Press,
Seattle, 2001.
The Naked Ape, Desmond Morris.
Dell, New York, 1994.
Solitude, Anthony Storr. Ballantine,
New York, 1989.

picture credits

The publisher would like to thank everyone who made the photography for this book possible.

All Photographs by Chris Tubbs
Key: a=above, b=below, c=center, l=left, r=right

1 Phil Lapworth's treehouse near Bath, UK; 2 Vermont Shack/Ross Anderson, anderson architects; 3 The Stone House in the country in Skane, Sweden; 4–7 Jonathan Adler's and Simon Doonan's house on Shelter Island near New York designed by Schefer Design; 8 Jenny Makepeace's house in Dorset, UK; 16bl Daniel Jasiak's home near Biarritz; 16–17a A house in Ramatuelle, St. Tropez; 16–17b Jonathan Adler's and Simon Doonan's house on Shelter Island near New York designed by Schefer Design; 17al Mike and Deborah Geary's beach house in Dorset, UK; 17ar A house in Ramatuelle, St. Tropez; 17bl Daniel Jasiak's home near Biarritz; 18–23 Jonathan Adler's and Simon Doonan's house on Shelter Island near New York designed by Schefer Design; 24, 26–27 Vadim Jean's Thames sailing barge in London; 28–33: Clara Baillie's house on the Isle of Wight; 34–39 A house in Ramatuelle, St. Tropez; 41–47 Daniel Jasiak's home near Biarritz; 48–53 Mike and Deborah Geary's beach house in Dorset, UK; 60–61b Daniel Jasiak's home near Biarritz; 61ar Mike Taitt's railroad wagon in Scotland; 61al Vermont Shack/Ross Anderson, anderson architects; 61br Maureen Kelly's house in the Catskills, New York; 62–65 Phil Lapworth's treehouse near Bath, UK; 66–73 Vermont Shack/Ross Anderson, anderson architects; 74–79 Nickerson-Wakefield House in upstate New York/anderson architects; 80–85 Mike Taitt's railroad wagon in Scotland; 88 & 92b Custom Airstream Trailer by Mark J. Marcinik, Greenmeadow Architects; 92a & 93bl The Stone House in the country in Skane, Sweden; 93ar&l A cottage in Connecticut designed by Benard M. Wharton; 93br La maison d'un antiquaire en art tribal et d'une créatrice de bijoux à Ramatuelle; 94–99 Custom Airstream Trailer by Mark J. Marcinik, Greenmeadow Architects; 100 & 102–103 A cottage in Connecticut designed by Benard M. Wharton; 104–107 La maison d'un antiquaire en art tribal et d'une créatrice de bijoux à Ramatuelle; 108–115 The Stone House in the country in Skane, Sweden; 118 Moens Dairyhouse in Dorset, UK owned by Marston Properties Ltd (020 7736 7133); 121bl Jenny Makepeace's house in Dorset, UK; 122bl & 123bl Moens Dairyhouse in Dorset, UK owned by Marston Properties Ltd (020 7736 7133); 123al Andrea McGarvie-Munn's garden; 125–129 Jenny Makepeace's house in Dorset, UK; 130–133 Moens Dairyhouse in Dorset, UK owned by Marston Properties Ltd (020 7736 7133); 134–137 Andrea McGarvie-Munn's garden; 139l Moens Dairyhouse in Dorset, UK owned by Marston Properties Ltd (020 7736 7133); 139c Nickerson-Wakefield House in upstate New York/anderson architects; 139r Daniel Jasiak's home near Biarritz; 140c Jonathan Adler's and Simon Doonan's house on Shelter Island near New York designed by Schefer Design; 140r Jenny Makepeace's house in Dorset, UK; 144 Nickerson-Wakefield House in upstate New York/anderson architects; endpapers Jonathan Adler's and Simon Doonan's house on Shelter Island near New York designed by Schefer Design.

acknowledgments

I want to say a big thank you to Alison Starling, Sophie Bevan, Gabriella Le Grazie, and everyone else at RPS who has worked so hard to produce this book. I am indebted to Chris Tubbs for his beautiful photography and ability to instantly capture the spirit of the book so perfectly. I would also like to thank Ali Watkinson for her excellent and thoughtful writing; Nicky Peters and Katie Ebben for their help in styling for the book; and Ben Kendrick for his suggestions.

A huge thanks to all the people who have let us photograph their private hideaways; without them it wouldn't have happened.

Patience is a virtue that I don't have a lot of, but my husband Rupert does. For that I want to thank him and big hugs. Thank you, too, to my sister Fiona for all her ideas, and to my mother and father for their inspiration.

Chris Tubbs would like to thank the following for their help, generosity and time: Jo Denbury and all at RPS for letting me work on such a fantastic project. Nicki Peters, Andrea McGarvie-Munn, and Chris Brooks for their help. Luis, Steve, and Nigel for their support, Dominique for her understanding. A big thank you to those who welcomed us into their wonderful homes.